I Support Anti-Racism To Create A Beautiful World

Kids Coloring Activity Book

This book belongs to

....

I Support Anti-Racism To Create A Beautiful World : Kids Coloring Activity Book (Anti Racist Children's Books)

ISBN: 9798653424144

Note: **The back page of each coloring page is <u>blank</u> to <u>prevent ink bleed</u> into the next illustration**

BE THE CHANGE
YOU WISH TO SEE

KIDS COLORING BOOK THEME

SAY BYE BYE TO RACISM

FRIENDSHIP IS FAR BETTER THAN RACISM

I'M A GOOD
HUMAN BEING

SHALL WE STUDY TOGETHER?

LET'S PLAY TOGETHER

SHARING IS CARING

FRIENDS FOREVER?

BE THE CHANGE
YOU WANT

LESS HATE MORE LOVE

ALWAYS BE
SOMEONE'S HOPE

I'LL BE THERE FOR YOU

BE LIKE A GOOD NEIGHBOR

HUMANITY IS KINDNESS

NO COLOR IS SPECIAL.
ALL ARE EQUAL

LET'S PLAY TOGETHER

PEACE AND HUMANITY IS MY RACE

QUIT RACISM

WE ALL ARE EQUAL

WE ARE HERE TO
BALANCE THE WORLD

RACISM AND HATE HAVE
NO PLACE HERE

COLOR DON'T DECIDE YOUR NATURE

ALWAYS BE KIND

CHOOSE HUMANITY
ALWAYS

YOU CANNOT WIN,
IF YOU ARE NOT A
GOOD HUMAN

I BELIEVE IN HUMANITY

ANTI-RACISM
STARTS AT HOME

IF YOU HAVE TO
CHOOSE, CHOOSE
HUMANITY FIRST

ALL ARE EQUAL

HUMANITY SHOULD
BE OUR RACE

Colorful
Floral Patterns
For
Beautiful Minds

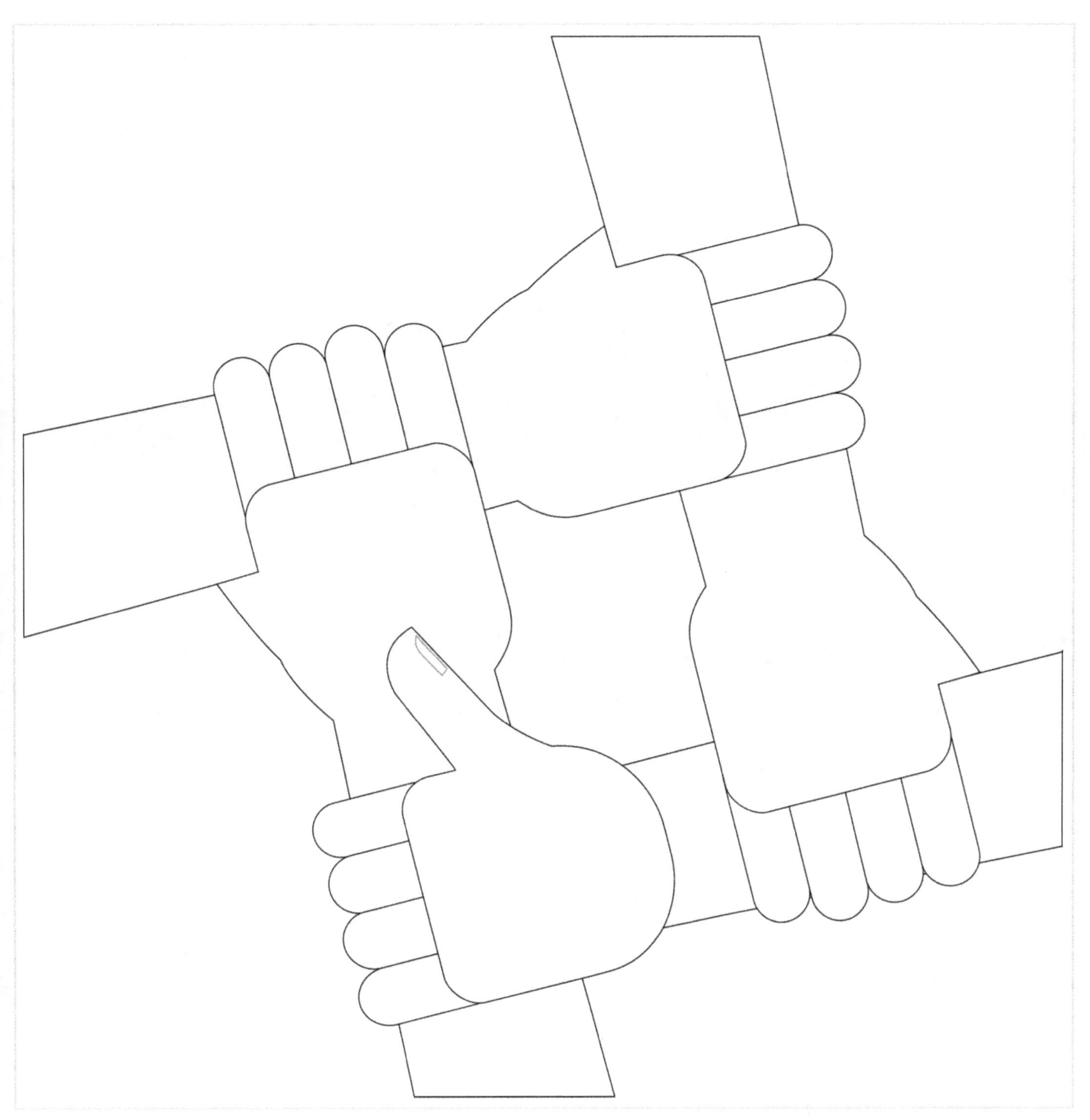

TOGETHER WERE STRONG

TOGETHER WE RISE